Leadership Resilience in Conflict

Sandra Cobbin

Trainer and Mediator

GROVE BOOKS LIMITED
RIDLEY HALL RD CAMBRIDGE CB3 9HU

Contents

Acknowledgments

With thanks to those whose stories are included in this book, from whom I have learned so much.
With thanks to Steve for your constant support and encouragement.

First Impression October 2015
ISSN 2041-0972
ISBN 978 1 85174 953 9

Introduction: Leadership Resilience in Times of Conflict

On a time management course for clergy I ran, I found that over 30% of those attending the course were leading in a context of heightened conflict. As we talked about what was happening, it became clear that hints and tips for managing time would make little or no difference to their effectiveness without also building their resilience as leaders in the midst of conflict.

This Grove booklet is not about conflict. Nor is it about leadership resilience. Its focus is leadership resilience in conflict. I want to offer a number of skills and tools to help leaders sustain their leadership when relationships are conflictual, emotions run high and behaviours are destructive. I have included stories, which I hope will bring the ideas to life. Each chapter ends with some questions to reflect upon.

I asked leaders from a range of contexts, all of whom have experienced heightened tensions and conflict: 'What would you say to a leader leading in a time of conflict?' Their responses are scattered through the book; I hope you find them helpful.

Facing a time of conflict, particularly as a leader, can be reminiscent of Shadrach, Meshach and Abednego. The leader walks into a fiery furnace of conflict, sometimes a conflict of which they are a part and sometimes a conflict between others, hoping that they will find divine help (Daniel 3). I want this book to encourage you in that hope; to equip you for the heat of a fiery furnace.

Where is God in this?

Resilience as a leader in a time of conflict is helped by a theological understanding of conflict. All too often conflict between Christians is seen as frustrating, embarrassing, or simply a waste of time. Conflict is seen as a distraction, absorbing time and energy that could be better used in the work of the gospel. Rarely does our theology of conflict enable us to see the possibilities for transformation that conflict offers. In the darkness, brokenness and messiness of conflict there is an opportunity to discover God's creativity, reconciliation and grace at work.

In his talk to the Faith in Conflict Conference at Coventry Cathedral in 2013, the Rev'd Dr Sam Wells challenged the view of many Christians that to engage with disagreement and conflict is a wasteful distraction from the main work of the church.[1] He asserted that engaging with conflict *is* the gospel. Christians are people who have been and are being reconciled to God. Conflict offers an opportunity for us to be part of the work of the gospel, the reconciliation of all things through Jesus Christ (2 Cor 5.17–19).

Disagreement and conflict are woven through the Bible, from the dispute about an apple in the Garden of Eden to dramatic and violent battles in John's vision recorded in the Book of Revelation. The Bible tells stories of conflict within families, between friends and colleagues, between nations and rulers. It tells of how the early church navigated potentially divisive issues such as circumcision and food offered to idols (Acts 15), gives advice about how to speak and listen (Jas 1.19–20), and offers models for dealing with conflict (for example, Matt 18.15–20).

Ultimately the Bible is a story about God's transforming grace, which weaves its way like a golden thread through stories of hatred, murder, lies and deceit. The conflict between King David, Uriah and Bathsheba is transformed by God's thread of grace, which brings Solomon to the throne. The conflict between Sarah and Hagar is transformed by God's thread of grace, as God meets with Hagar and blesses her son Ishmael with many descendants. Situations of conflict rarely become neat and tidy as a result of God's grace-move. Instead, amidst the messiness a new future opens up, shaped by the conflict, but no longer defined by it. It is a future in which there is new life and light, made possible by God's transforming grace.

In Jesus we meet God's transformational, redemptive grace face to face. Jesus' death and resurrection mark the beginning of all things being made new. As God's image bearers, and as reconciled people, we are called to be part of God's grace-filled reconciliation in a world of brokenness, working towards God's kingdom breaking into this hurting world. As we pray 'Your kingdom come,' we are invited to be active in God's reconciliation of all things through Jesus.

> Quotation from a leader: 'Repeatedly tell yourself that you are an apprentice in the workshop alongside the risen Christ and not a caretaker to an absent landlord.'

Being involved in God's reconciliation of all things can be a task full of hope for a different future, reminiscent of Jesus' and Peter's walk on the beach (John 21.15–19) or Jacob seeing 'the face of God' in his long-estranged brother's face (Gen 33.10). Being involved in God's reconciliation of all things can resonate with a Friday afternoon outside Jerusalem two thousand years ago, as we stand in the pain and darkness of conflict, sharing in the agony and cost of the reconciliation of all things.

> Quotation from a leader: 'The pathological avoidance of conflict leads to high levels of anxiety, stagnation and decline. Conflict need not lead inevitably to division, though it is rarely, if ever, painless.'

To Reflect Upon

In Sam Wells' talk, referred to above, he suggests that reconciliation is not about the replacement of conflict with peace. Rather, reconciliation is about the transfiguration of conflict into glory.[2] How might our task of leadership be different if we see it not as changing conflict to peace, but rather as being part of God's grace-filled reconciling of all things, transforming conflict into glory?

Resilience is…having a theology of conflict.

Resilience is…playing our part as God reconciles all things.

3   Learn to Judge How Tense it Really Is

I had the privilege of facilitating a seminar group at an annual conference for Church of England and Methodist safeguarding advisors. I asked my group to describe what indicators of conflict they saw in churches they were working with. They described: evidence of 'us' and 'them,' emphatic language of absolutes, information being withheld, 'information-gossiping' and a low trust of 'them.' They mapped these indicators of conflict onto Speed Leas' model of escalating conflict.[3]

As they did this there was a sense of surprise. The model showed that the patterns of behaviour and language they had identified and the 'feel' of the churches were normal in a time of conflict and heightened anxiety.

There was also a sense of optimism. The model opened up a discussion about how the safeguarding advisor, working with others in the church, could begin to de-escalate the conflict and invite the congregation to journey to a place of less intense conflict and anxiety.

Most of us will instinctively assess the intensity of a disagreement or conflict that we are involved in or that is happening around us. This subjective assessment will be influenced, amongst other things, by the extent to which the conflict involves us, what we think and feel in response to what is going on, our personal experience of conflict in the past and our personal conflict resilience.

Speed Leas' model of escalating conflict uses four indicators to assess the level of conflict:

- The goals of those involved;
- The behaviours of people involved;
- The language being used;
- The group make-up of those involved.

The advantage of a model is that it enables the leader to make an objective assessment of the conflict level: which step on the staircase the conflict is on. The objective assessment using various criteria helps build resilience in the leader by normalizing the behaviours they are experiencing. It sets the conflict within a framework of escalation and de-escalation and helps the leader identify appropriate responses to the conflict. The model enables the leader to identify possible interventions in order to address issues so that the conflict might be transformed into glory. And finally, it enables the leader to know when they may need help.

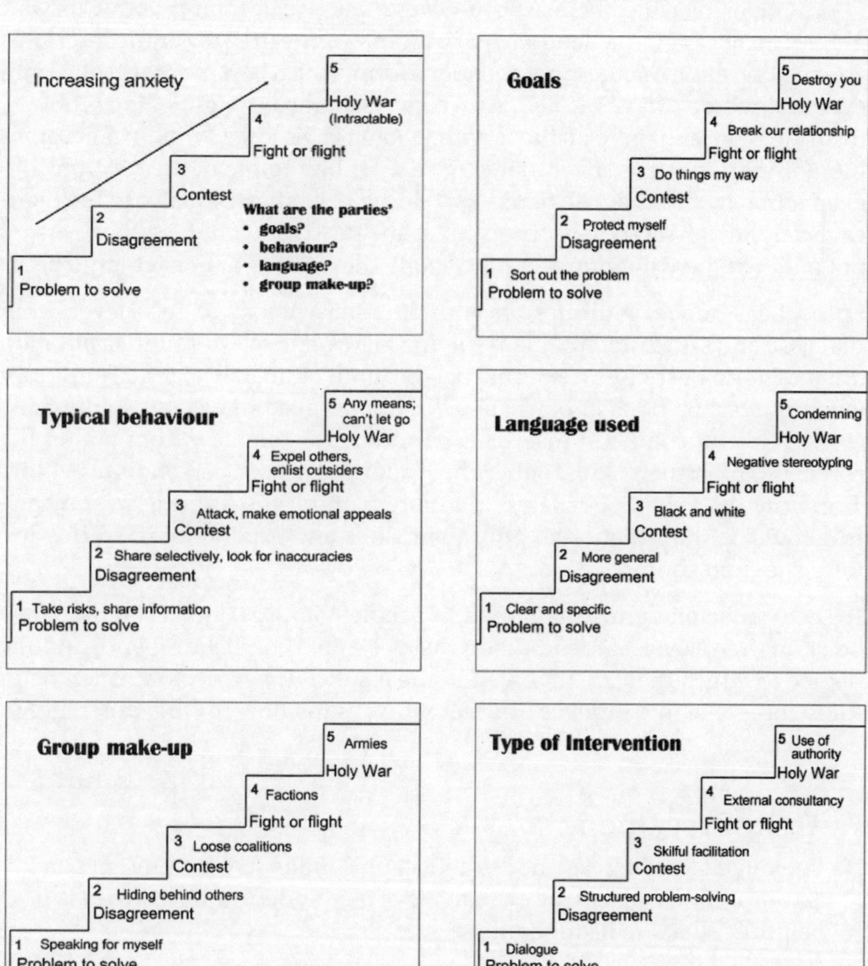

Fig 1 Speed Leas: Levels of Conflict
(Taken from 'Transforming Church Conflict' course Manual,
Bridge Builders Ministries[4])

Speed Leas' model shows that as conflict escalates our priorities and behaviours change. Initially we are all trying to solve the problem by sharing information and working together; our language is inclusive and our focus is the problem; relationships are cooperative and open. As the conflict escalates our focus moves away from the problem to the people with whom we disagree. We become more cautious about sharing information; we look for errors in information given by others. As conflict escalates we hear more about 'us' and 'them'; increasingly the language of absolutes is heard. As conflict escalates and relationships change loose coalitions form, which become more solid until eventually 'sides' have formed. As we increasingly lose sight of the problem, focusing more and more on those with whom we disagree, 'winning' becomes more important to us. Eventually, we are willing to break the relationship, even if that means that one of us has to leave. If conflict escalates to the highest level the only acceptable outcome is the destruction of the other person; not only will they not minister here again, they will not minister anywhere.

Speed Leas' model indicates appropriate interventions at each level, from dialogue and structured problem solving at lower levels, through facilitation offered internally or by an external person, until ultimately external authority (such as a bishop or chair of trustees, for example) administers a solution. At lower levels of conflict it may be appropriate for someone from within the context to offer their skills, either the leader or another person from within. The more the conflict escalates, the more helpful it is to bring in someone from outside the situation to offer their skills and experience in addressing the issues and conflict.

It is worth remembering that different people within a conflict situation may be at different levels depending on their personal conflict resilience and the degree to which they are involved in the conflict. It is, therefore, often helpful to intervene in a number of different ways to allow for this difference in experience.

To Reflect Upon

Looking at Speed Leas' model, reflect on conflict in your present context or in other places. How realistic is the model? In what ways is it helpful? What are its limitations?

Resilience is…understanding levels of conflict and responding appropriately.

Recognize Patterns of Anxiety

4

A new director of a charity realized the department head, who had run the organization in the interim, was demonstrating high anxiety. She noticed he had a number of anxiety habits that increased anxiety in others, notably:

- Talking about his anxieties about the future;

- Selectively sharing information;

- Passing on things that people had said to him.

The new director realized she needed to resist the temptation to 'catch' his anxiety and react to it. She realized she needed to offer an emotionally mature response. She arranged a number of meetings with staff at which she spoke clearly about her role and expectations. She invited open discussion about issues. She remained calm and optimistic even as heightened emotion and anxiety were expressed. Very quickly she sensed a lowering of the level of anxiety in the organization. People said they appreciated her clarity about the future. Many people responded with emotional maturity, engaging constructively with issues faced by the charity. However, the anxiety of the department head increased. The director's reflection was that the department head coped with his high levels of personal anxiety through his anxiety habits, which transferred his anxiety to others. As the organization became less anxious in response to the clear, open and non-anxious leadership from the new director, his anxiety habits were no longer effective and his personal anxiety increased.

'Anxiety' can be a useful way of understanding what is happening within a group, organization or congregation. Anxiety indicates an increase in emotional intensity. It is helpful to imagine anxiety as an electric current passing between people. Think about the way anxiety passes through a herd of deer when one of them senses a predator. Perhaps you have seen anxiety pass through the people in your organization or congregation in a similar way? Here are two ways in which anxiety is passed, like a current, between people:

- *Anxiety generators*—generate a current of anxiety and emotion that they pass to others: 'I thought you ought to know…' 'I don't think we've got enough…' 'I'm not sure that'll work…'

The higher our personal anxiety and/or the anxiety of others the harder it is to respond with both head and heart. Here are three responses to heightened anxiety and emotion:

- *Emotional fusion*—we become overwhelmed by anxiety around us and lose sight of our own emotions and views. We might blame others for the way we feel. We might find ourselves holding opinions that we would not hold if our head and heart were in balance. We might find ways to pass on the anxiety we are absorbing from others in order to reduce the emotional discomfort we feel.

- *Emotional distance*—we withdraw emotionally and mentally from others. This may be a physical withdrawal too. We may find it hard to offer empathetic listening. We may not notice the emotion and anxiety of others; if we sense it we may withdraw from it. We may not notice the emotion we are feeling and its effect on our ability to think clearly.

- *Emotional maturity*—we maintain appropriate emotional connection and emotional distinctiveness. We respond with a balance of head and heart. We take responsibility for the way we feel and seek to ensure that our emotional responses do not overwhelm us or others. We are open about our views and opinions whilst listening to those held by others. We invite emotional maturity from others.

Developing emotional maturity is the journey of a lifetime. It is likely that each of us has triggers from our experience of life that make it harder in some situations to maintain emotional maturity. We react to a trigger, perhaps a tone of voice or particular behaviour, and find ourselves being overwhelmed into emotional fusion or pulling away into emotional distance.

Building resilience in conflict involves developing less anxious leadership, with emotional maturity that maintains a healthy balance of head and heart:

- We practice sustained, appropriate emotional empathy and connection to others, maintaining interest and openness towards them;

- We retain our emotional distinctiveness, being aware of our own emotions without them overwhelming us, and aware of the emotion of others without being overwhelmed by them;

- We remain curious rather than judgmental;

- We seek to understand, even when our own heightened emotion makes this difficult;

- We learn to listen to the words and feelings being expressed, even during heightened emotion from others and perhaps ourselves;

- We hit the inner pause button in our head so that we can be attentive to the other person rather than preparing a reply, retort or defence;

- We remain a calm, confident, emotionally distinctive person, who is clear about their role and is comfortable taking time to respond;

- We speak carefully and unambiguously, taking time to check that we have understood and are being understood.

The leader who wants to build their resilience in times of conflict needs to develop healthy personal anxiety habits and emotional maturity by doing the personal work of identifying their anxiety habits, understanding their roots and inviting God's grace-filled transformation. With practice we will learn to maintain emotional connection and distinctiveness, the balance of head and heart. As we learn to maintain and offer emotional maturity in times of conflict, we find that others respond with emotional maturity too.

To Reflect Upon

When anxiety and emotion have escalated, what are my personal anxiety habits? When others pass anxiety to me, do I absorb it, pass it on or am I able to remain emotionally distinctive? What are the anxiety habits in my church or organization? How do people deal with their personal anxiety? Who are the anxiety generators and boosters? Who is offering emotional maturity amidst anxiety?

Resilience is…recognizing anxiety moving like an electric current.

Resilience is…knowing my anxiety habits and inviting God to transform them.

5
Examine the Role Others Want to Give You

An experienced leader in the midst of heightened conflict realized that despite some of the faults of others he was responsible for the situation he was in and his reactions to it: 'How had I allowed myself to be controlled by others in such a devastating way?' Seeing his part in the conflict and realizing that God was at work changing him through the conflict provided important learning for him. 'I wouldn't wish to go through that level of escalated conflict again, but I am so glad I have.'

Whatever the source of conflict, when differences escalate, emotion and anxiety escalate too. Some people cope with their own anxiety and emotion by putting pressure on the leader to play a particular role in the conflict—rescuer, martyr, parent, fighter, survivor, to name but a few. The temptation to take up the roles others want the leader to have may be overt, or implied by how they behave. The leader who is unclear about their role is likely to find themselves taking up roles that are unsuitable and unhelpful, as listed above. A resilient leader is clear about their role, which can help them resist the inappropriate expectations of others.

The particular roles that attract us may be connected to our personal experience of conflict or our personal conflict style. They may also be shaped by our own brokenness and the needs within us that are fed by the expectations of others. It is important to understand how our experience of conflict as a child impacts upon us as adults. My family of origin had little open disagreement and only occasional outbursts of anger. This was a positive experience for me. I remember going for lunch at a friend's house where disagreement was encouraged. The lunchtime felt like a battle ground. I emerged exhausted and fearful for the future of their family relationships. As an adult I have found that my childhood experience did not equip me to engage in conflict in a healthy way. I have had to build personal resilience in times of heightened emotion and conflict in relationships. A key part of building that resilience has been awareness of the roles that I am tempted to take up, which often reflect something of my brokenness and need. It can be helpful for the leader to ask, 'What role am I being invited to take?' This question enables the leader to step outside the situation, with all its pressures and emotions, and assess what part they are being asked to play. Having identified the role or roles that others are expecting of them, the leader can decide whether that is appropriate. The greater clarity the leader has of their role within the organization or congregation, the easier it is to identify what others expect of them and how closely aligned that is to their sense of who they are and what they are there for. This focus and clarity enables the leader to choose to offer a clearly defined person, with a clear understanding of their role. It enables them to resist the temptation to be what others want them to be and instead to offer themselves.

> Quotation from a leader: 'Knowing who I am, what I am called to do and my purpose is vital.'

Under pressure it is demanding for a leader to retain a clear role that enables the leader to remain appropriately emotionally connected and emotionally distinctive. We are more likely to be able to do this if we pay attention to our own emotional responses and retain a healthy balance of head and heart responses to what is going on around us. We can offer an emotionally mature and less anxious presence. We are clear and unambiguous about the role we have.

To Reflect Upon

Which roles are most seductive to you? Why are these roles appealing? How might you develop emotional maturity to resist these roles when others offer them to you?

Resilience is…not having to accept the roles others assign to me.

Resilience is…looking for ways God is changing us.

Reflection on the Temptation of Jesus (Matt 4.1–11)

Jesus offers us a supreme example of a leader who remains emotionally mature and distinctive, not anxious in an interaction with a highly dysfunctional being!

- The tempter seeks to undermine Jesus' identity, purpose and calling.

- The tempter tries a variety of approaches to get a reaction from Jesus.

- The tempter is provocative, goading Jesus with half-truths.

- The tempter is personal, questioning Jesus' identity as the Son of God.

- The tempter is persistent; when one approach does not work the tempter tries another.

- Jesus does not absorb the anxiety being offered to him.

- Jesus does not absorb the responsibility to win the argument and prove the tempter wrong.

- Jesus does not get drawn into a need to defend himself, to attach the half-truths or to retreat from the tempter.

- Jesus remains focused on his Father.

- Jesus remains calm and emotionally distinctive.

- Jesus remains clear in his identity and purpose.

Tackle Triangles Differently

6

I was recently blind copied to an email, as a result of which I knew something significant about the recipient of the email that I had not known before. Because I had been blind copied they did not know I knew. The sender had created an unhealthy triangle between the three of us. My anxiety and emotion escalated. I felt very uncomfortable and frustrated. I decided to re-triangle. I went to see the sender of the email. I explained my frustration about being blind copied into the email. I listened to the reasons why the sender had blind copied me. We talked about the impact of the unhealthy triangle. The sender of the email took responsibility for their actions, decided to speak with the recipient, explain what had happened and why, and apologized for their action. I offered to meet with the recipient. The recipient expressed gratitude that I had met with them as it demonstrated my view of them had not changed as a result of what I now knew.

Triangles are familiar in a number of therapeutic models. In this book I am referring to the way that family systems theory uses triangles.[5] A triangle is formed when a third person (individual, group or organization) is invited into a relationship. Triangles can be healthy or unhealthy.

Healthy triangles are constructive, positive and do not seek to pass on anxiety or responsibility.

For example:

- Two friends spend the day together; on returning home one of them shares the enjoyment of her day with her husband.

- A man is having a difficult time with his boss; he meets up with a friend to talk through what is happening as a way of processing the issues and getting ideas of what to do about his boss.

- A volunteer has an issue with another volunteer; they talk with a trusted friend in order to decide how to respond.

Counselling, coaching, spiritual direction and other helpful support relationships offer healthy triangles.

Unhealthy triangles are not constructive or positive; the aim is to pass on anxiety and responsibility and lower one's own feeling of emotional discomfort.

For example:

- Two friends spend the day together; on returning home one of them moans to her husband about how boring her friend is and what an awful day she has had.

- A man is having a difficult time with his boss; he meets up with a friend to criticize his boss; he is not interested in any discussion about how he could address the situation.

- A volunteer is upset by something another volunteer has said; they talk to a number of other volunteers about what has happened, seeking support and affirmation.

In times of escalated conflict and heightened anxiety unhealthy triangles are an effective way of passing on the electric current of anxiety. Triangles enable people to lower their personal discomfort by passing it to others. The leader is often a focus for unhealthy triangles.

I was explaining triangles to a group of curates when one of the curates exclaimed, 'But I thought it was my job to take people's anxieties.' When the leader takes on the anxiety and responsibility of another person they accept the invitation from them to take on a role, for example, parent or saviour. When leaders absorb the anxiety of others, they carry burdens of anxiety and responsibility that more appropriately belong to others. As a result, other people do not have the opportunity to develop emotional maturity by learning to deal with their own anxiety or emotion. Nor do they have the opportunity to develop their ability to take responsibility for dealing with issues in relationships.

Let us look at a scenario. Does this sound familiar?

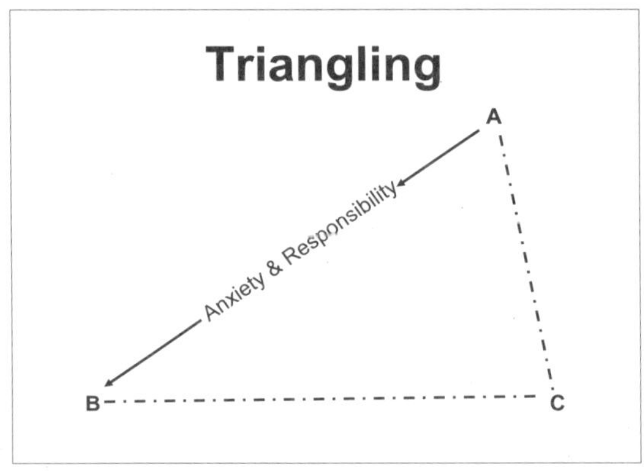

One of the most creative resilience skills a leader can develop in times of conflict is their understanding of triangling and their ability to re-triangle. Re-Triangling is the way we turn an unhealthy triangle into a healthy triangle.

Let us look at what re-triangling might look like in this scenario.

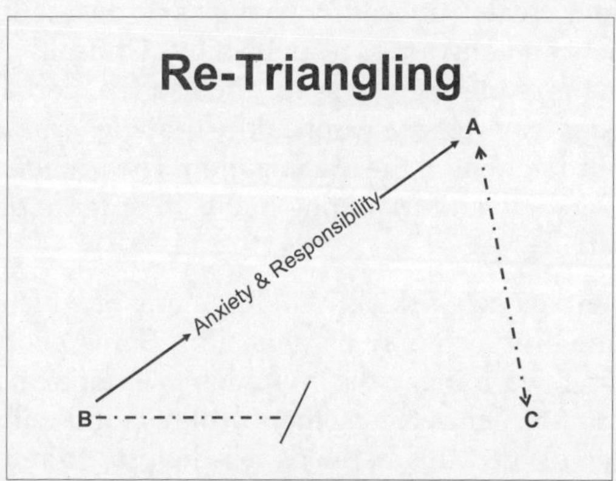

- The leader, *B*, resists the temptation to absorb *A*'s anxiety and responsibility;

- *B* retains emotionally mature leadership by passing the anxiety and responsibility back to *A*, inviting emotional maturity from *A*;

- *B* asks whether *A* has spoken to *C*, why the issue bothers *A* and perhaps how *A* might be less bothered by *C*.

The leader, *B*, does not absorb *A*'s anxiety or the responsibility to speak to *C*.

Instead, *B* invites *A* to a more emotionally mature response in which *A* acknowledges their emotional anxiety about *C*.

A is encouraged to take responsibility to speak to *C* rather than to *speak about them* to *B*.

Skills of re-triangling build the resilience of a leader facing conflict. The leader's skills of re-triangling potentially build resilience in others as they respond to the invitation to develop their emotional maturity. Re-triangling may be an invitation for a person to respond differently from their personal anxiety habits of a lifetime. Sometimes it may be appropriate for the leader to coach them as they develop emotional maturity, supporting them as they practise taking responsibility for feelings and actions they have previously passed to others. Sometimes it may be appropriate for the leader to create a healthy triangle by mediating a difficult conversation between two people who have been speaking about each other rather than to each other.

Sometimes a leader creates unhealthy triangles to deal with their own uncomfortable anxiety and unwanted responsibility. Unhealthy triangles might reinforce the role the leader perceives for themselves, perhaps as martyr or saviour. If the leader tends to create unhealthy triangles, this way of behaving is likely to be replicated within the organization. The resilient leader will pay attention to their anxiety and triangling habits in order to develop personal emotional maturity.

We are all in a complex network of triangles, many of which will be healthy and positive, some of which may be unhealthy. Some people will respond well to re-triangling, warming to the invitation to emotional maturity and to take responsibility for themselves. Others will respond with resistance and heightened anxiety. When this happens it is helpful to remember that the leader invites emotional maturity; the other person can refuse that invitation. When the invitation is not accepted it is important the leader remains emotionally distinctive and emotionally connected, maintaining a healthy triangle in which they do not absorb or react to the anxiety, do not take inappropriate responsibility and resist the temptation to accept the invitation to take inappropriate roles.

To Reflect Upon

To what extent are you part of unhealthy triangles? How might you develop skills of re-triangling? How often do you create unhealthy triangles as a way of dealing with your own anxiety? How might you develop personally so that you create fewer unhealthy triangles?

Resilience is…re-triangling.

Resilience is…being a person who creates healthy triangles.

Reflection on the Woman Caught in Adultery (John 8.1–11)

The Pharisees bring the women caught in adultery to Jesus, creating an unhealthy triangle.

Jesus re-triangles.

He does not absorb their heightened anxiety and emotion. Instead, he bends down to write in the sand. He is calm, emotionally connected and distinctive and not anxious.

Notice how initially the Pharisees' emotion escalates in response to Jesus' calmness.

Jesus does not accept the invitation to take the role of judge with the responsibility to decide whether or not the woman should be stoned. Instead he invites emotional maturity from the Pharisees: 'Let anyone among you who is without sin be the first to throw a stone at her.'

We are told that the eldest go away first; they accept the invitation to emotional maturity and responsibility.

Once they have all left, Jesus turns to the woman. He re-triangles: 'Has no-one condemned you?'

Jesus invites emotional maturity from the woman: 'Go your way, and from now on do not sin again.'

7. The Importance of Story

A vicar wanted to remove a couple of pews to make room for push chairs because of a growing Messy Church. The reaction of the congregation was intense, fierce and vitriolic. The vicar discovered his predecessor had removed a couple of pews to make room for a music group when introducing a new style of worship. This had led to fierce disagreement; eventually a number of significant people had left the church and not returned. The conflict was not addressed; it was swept under the carpet and forgotten about. When the new vicar suggested removing a couple of pews, the unresolved anger, hurt, betrayal and grief of the earlier conflict re-emerged.

Congregations and organizations have a shared story, which when understood can help them make sense of present conflict and open up the possibility of choosing a different future.When a leader is new they are usually told some elements of the story of the place and people. Sometimes the shared story includes something painful or difficult that remains hidden. Perhaps the congregation is ashamed. They may believe they have dealt with it and moved on. They may believe it is not relevant. This hidden or secret part of the story can be difficult for a new leader to discover. However, it is not unusual for the bit of the story that has been swept under the carpet to trip people up, perhaps years later.

Seeing off the Minister

A minister found he was criticized and argued with at every turn. PCC meetings were an exhausting ordeal. He found it difficult to get clear information or find out who was responsible for what in the church. He discovered that the last two ministers had experienced something similar. Neither had lasted more than three years. Eventually he discovered that over twenty years ago a minister had been sent to prison for sexual offences against children. The next minister had left because of an affair with someone in the church. As the minister discovered these secrets he realized very little had been done to help the congregation address these traumatic events. Things had been swept under the carpet and the congregation had apparently moved on. However, he began to realize there was an unconscious agreement that they would not let a minister hurt or betray them again. They collaborated to develop a pattern of seeing off new ministers before they could be hurt by them.

Shared storytelling can involve the whole congregation/organization, or a smaller group such as the leadership team, council or board. Those involved are invited to tell the story, to celebrate all that they are thankful for and to name the things about which there is regret or hurt. It is helpful to look for repeated patterns in the story. Sometimes it is appropriate for the leader to facilitate shared storytelling. Sometimes it is more appropriate for an external facilitator to do so.

A Story About a Story

A number of people had left the church because they disagreed with the new minister's approach. One of the things the church did to address this situation was hold a storytelling event. They placed a long piece of lining paper on the wall. Each person drew a picture of themselves on the date they arrived at the church. Then, using words, pictures and symbols they recorded key dates and events in the story of the church from the earliest living memories of the people in the room. They recorded joys and sadness, celebration and regret. Once they had finished, they were invited to reflect on their story in light of the current issues and look for patterns. One of the leaders suddenly exclaimed, 'We're doing this to ourselves!' It was a turning point in their understanding about the way they were reacting to their new minister. This moment of seeing patterns in the story led to an honest, open and positive discussion about their current situation. Rather than see this minister off, they began to explore how they might enable this minster to stay by addressing some of the repeated patterns. They began to explore how they could choose a different future.

A leader builds resilience by being able to tell their personal story of joy and pain, and by understanding the patterns of darkness and light in their story and how God's grace has been at work. Out of the experience of finding God in their personal story a leader can lead others as they look for the patterns of darkness and light in their shared story, encouraging them to look for God's grace. They can be invited to choose a different future, no longer defined by the past, but shaped by God's grace that transforms conflict into glory.

To Reflect Upon

How might collective storytelling help an organization address repeated issues? What are the risks and limitations of this way of identifying and understanding issues?

Resilience is…seeing patterns in the story.

Resilience is…allowing God's grace to lead us into a different future.

---

8 Sabbath Rest and Other Good Habits

Leaders who choose to respond appropriately to conflict in their context by offering and inviting emotional maturity will benefit from a range of resilience habits that will sustain them over time, as the transformation of conflict by grace into God's glory can take months or years.

> Quotation from a leader: 'I find spiritual disciplines really hard and still do when I feel emotionally churned up. It is so easy to drift in our spiritual disciplines, or to use them to solely reflect or pray about the conflict. "Be still and know that I am the Lord" (Ps 46.10), this verse comes in the midst of huge turmoil and upheaval, but there is a place where we can find our centre, a stillness and a calmness in the midst of the conflict and turmoil. Even if I find it hard to get to that place, I find knowing that it is possible is an encouragement.'

In this chapter I want to concentrate on five good habits of leadership resilience that will resource a leader for times of conflict:

- Forgiveness
- Loneliness
- Laughter
- Prayer
- Sabbath rest

Forgiveness

At some point conflict between Christians stumbles over the knotty problem of forgiveness. One way leaders build resilience for times of conflict is by accepting the forgiveness offered by God and being transformed by God's grace. Such a leader then embarks on the sometimes hard work of allowing the forgiveness they have received from God to overflow to others, in the hope of grace-filled transformation. They draw on their own story, which informs them as they lead others in an appropriate and timely way on the journey to forgiveness. Forgiveness is central to our faith, but it takes practice, it can be difficult and it often takes time.

Loneliness

Leaders often speak of the loneliness of their role, especially when they have few peers or colleagues, or perhaps close family and friends are geographically far away. In times of conflict, the role of the leader can be even more lonely—people are speaking about us, confidences are broken, we are not sure who we can trust and no one else seems concerned about the destructive behaviours of others. We are trying to bring about change in the way people are with each other and nothing much seems to be changing. Our friends in ministry seem to be having more fun and more success than we are.

Create Healthy Triangles

It is not unusual for the leader's spiritual walk to be impacted negatively by a situation of conflict. Prayer is difficult. God seems distant. The conflict becomes the lens through which the leader sees everything. It is not unusual for a leader to feel their skills are insufficient for the task of leading in the conflict. Establishing relationships of support builds resilience in leadership; this is even more important during conflict. In these healthy triangles the leader can talk about what is happening, about the people involved and about their experience of leading in a time of conflict. The healthy triangle is a place for support, sense-making, developing skills and exploring options.

For example:

- A mentor, a leader who offers their experience and wisdom;

- A spiritual director, to whom you can make yourself accountable for your spiritual well-being, disciplines and maturity;

- A coach, experienced in supporting leaders in times of conflict;

- A peer group for prayer and support;

- One or two local leaders with whom you can talk through what is happening and who will pray with and for you.

Leaders can build resilience through relationships with family and close friends. Finding time for these relationships can be challenging when things are going well; it can be even more difficult when leading in a time of conflict. Sometimes the leader feels it is not possible to take a day off or go away when relationships are fraught. The leader needs to be watchful that they have not taken on an inappropriate role, perhaps assuming the responsibility for holding the church together.

Quotation from a leader: 'The hardest part is not to take what is said or done personally; find someone outside the situation who you can bounce ideas off, talk to, who will listen without passing judgment on either side and who will support you as you go through the conflict.

To Reflect Upon

When was the last time I was restored by time with people I love and trust and who love and trust me? What stops me from spending time with the life-giving people I know? What can I change so that I have time with them?

Laughter

An absence of laughter usually accompanies heightened anxiety and tension. In times of conflict there is a risk that the leader spends all their time in intense encounters. The resilient leader will seek out people who bring laughter, as a way of being personally restored. This might be half an hour of a Michael Macintyre DVD or spending time with a friend who makes you laugh.

An ability to laugh can bring a light touch to tense conversations; paradox and appropriate humour can lighten a tense situation. However, humour can increase tension if it is badly timed, especially when it comes out of our own anxiety as a way to reduce the discomfort we feel. Laughter that is offered from an open and non-anxious person can be life-giving in times of tension, a gift to others.

> ### To Reflect Upon
> When was the last time the council or board laughed? What might enable them to laugh together?

Prayer

A vicar asked for help with his management of time. As he began to talk about how he spent his time it became clear that he was leading in a context of heightened tension and conflictual relationships. He was on the receiving end of vicious things said and done by people on the PCC and in the wider congregation. He said he could not remember the last time he had prayed other than in front of a congregation. He felt abandoned by God. Before addressing tips for time management, he decided to pay attention to his rhythm of prayer. He decided that once in the coming week he would drive to a nearby scenic spot with his prayer book. He might pray. He might just sit. This was his first life-giving step towards building resilience in the context of conflict. Gradually, over the following months, he re-established a rhythm of personal prayer and prayer with others that resourced him for his role of costly leadership.

Busyness is often the blight of the modern leader, and prayer is often a casualty of busyness. When a congregation or organization is in the midst of conflict there seems to be even more to do. Sustaining a habit of regular prayer can be even more challenging.

> ### To Reflect Upon
> Am I too busy to pray? Are all my prayers about the conflict and tensions? Does God seem far away or absent?

To what extent are my habits of prayer sustaining me? What can I change in order to develop habits of prayer that will sustain me more? What is the first step towards that change?

Sabbath Rest

A leader established a rhythm of a seventh-weekly Sabbath rest. She put a line through every seventh week in her diary. Aside from her regular commitments to lead worship she did not attend meetings. She used this Sabbath week to create space. She visited the people for whom the need for a visit would never be urgent and who would appreciate a visit. She took time to walk and pray. She cleared paperwork and administration that she did not get round to normally. She had tea with her children every day. She found refreshment, restoration and new perspective from this rhythm of seventh-weekly Sabbath rest.

Regular Sabbath rest is important for refreshment and perspective, especially in a time of conflict. The uncluttered time and space of Sabbath enables the leader to step back from the intensity of the tensions and to see what God is doing. In times of heightened anxiety and conflict it can be difficult to see where God is at work. Sabbath enables the leader to look for God at work in their personal story and in the shared life of the church or organization they lead.

In stepping away there is also a keeping quiet so that the leader's inner noise gradually quietens, enabling them to listen for and hear the still small voice of God. Sabbath is not about busyness at different tasks. Sabbath can be a time to walk slowly, to sit for a long time, to do nothing.

To Reflect Upon

What is your rhythm of Sabbath rest? To what extent does it sustain you? Where are the times and places of stillness and quiet?

Not Now

At the start of this book I mentioned that a leader engaging with conflict is resonant with walking into the fiery furnace and hoping to find divine help there. Joining in with God's work of the reconciliation of all things can be costly and demanding. The sustained emotional maturity required of the resilient leader in the midst of conflict takes intention and energy, focus and determination. A wise leader recognizes when they do not have the necessary resilience to face a specific conflict. It may be that doing nothing is fine. However, if something needs to be done they look for support personally to build their own resilience. Or they may invite others to intervene instead.

Resilience is…laughter.

Resilience is…companions; do not journey alone.

Resilience is…praying even when God cannot be found, because maybe today he can be.

9 In Conclusion

In Paul's letter to his friend Philemon we see the leader Paul with his sleeves rolled up and arms outstretched standing in the mud and mire of a broken, unforgiving relationship. In this letter Paul gets dirty in the real-life messiness of other people's conflict, as he urges the two protagonists to grapple with the hard work of the reconciliation of all things in Christ.

Paul recognizes the profound risk that Onesimus will take in returning to the master from whom he has run away.

Paul invites Philemon to reimagine his relationship with Onesimus no longer as a slave, but as a brother.

Although there is no mention of forgiveness, Paul invites Onesimus and Philemon to take the costly and risky journey towards each other. He invites them to a reimagined relationship that is impossible without forgiveness.

Paul urges them to be part of God's reconciling of all things in Jesus. He invites them to allow the grace of God to transform their hearts and their relationship from conflict to glory.

Notes

1   The Rev'd Dr Sam Wells, 'The Exasperating Patience of God,' Talk at Faith in Conflict Conference, Coventry Cathedral, April 2013.

2   The Rev'd Dr Sam Wells, 'The Exasperating Patience of God,' Talk at Faith in Conflict Conference, Coventry Cathedral, April 2013.

3   Speed Leas, 'Model of Escalating Conflict,' *Transforming Church Conflict Manual* (London: Bridge Builders, 2015) pp 101ff.

4   Speed Leas, 'Model of Escalating Conflict,' *Transforming Church Conflict Manual* (London: Bridge Builders, 2015) pp 101ff.

5   Edwin H Friedman, *A Failure of Nerve* (New York: Seabury Books, 2007) p 57ff.